The Craft of Stand-up Comedy

By

Julie Sandoval

If we lived in a perfect world this book and stand-up comedy would be pointless. But we don't live in a perfect world and our lives are far from perfect. We have all had our share of disappointments, sadness and struggles. I know personally, I have found myself alone and awake at night, wondering how I was going to face yet another day. At those times, I am so grateful for stand-up comedy. Stand-up comedy has been the gift that turns my tears, fears and weakness into laughter. I'm not the world's greatest stand-up comedian, but I am the world's greatest Stand-up comedy teacher. I want to teach the world to laugh. This is my gift to you.

Julie Sandoval

Hagerstown, Pasadena, Palm Coast

The Craft of Stand-up Comedy

Contents

Part Two Continued

- ➤ The 8 Questions of Comedy Writing Exercises
- ➤ Comedy Shorthand
- ➤ The Rule of Three
- ➤ Comedy Description
- ➤ Creating Bits and Creating Bits Exercise
- ➤ Organizing Your Set and Organizing Your Set Exercise
- ➤ Making Transitions

Part Three

- ➤ How to Test Material
- ➤ Practicing Your Set
- ➤ Open Mics
- ➤ The Three Secret Ingredients of Stand-up Comedy Performance
- ➤ Voices
- ➤ Action
- ➤ Feelings
- ➤ Timing
- ➤ Stage Persona
- ➤ Sharing the Stage With YOU!

Acknowledgments

A grateful heart is definitely a happy heart. I am so overjoyed by the many incredible people who have touched my life. I personally believe God moves us across a chess board we can't see. He moves people in and out of our lives and every meeting has meaning. Some meetings you remember, some fade as time passes. Some are unimportant and some are life changing. Thank-you Michael Schwartz for a meeting that changed a life. Thank you for sharing your love of laughter with me. And Thank-you for helping me to find the courage to take that all so important first step.

I am so thankful to my students. The hours and hours of belly roll laughter has absolutely added years to my life and life to my years. Much heartfelt thanks to: Ira Bershoski, Brian Chaney, Mike St. Clair, David Sharpe, Spencer Sharpe, Dr. Deana Dixon, David Hodge, Robin Knott, Kahlil Nelson, Caylee Norrod, Nathaniel Zito, Grace Summer, Mark Akita, Quamaine Jones, Tremaine Jones, Carlos Aguilar, David Beadle, Richard Chou, Jason Contreras, Carol Jackson, Kitty Kroger, Trish Ryan, Laura Flores-Shaw, Mark Sweeney, Mike Laird, Dhurpatti Mangar, Claire Savage, Sean Shroff, David Carlberg, Steve Cipriani, Jane Fuller, Wyatt Gray, Kip Harper, Jesse Munoz, Joseph Olivares, Tom Edwards, Velma Butler, Paul Hermelin, Pamela Huley, Michael Johnson, Grace So, Kirkland Walls, Kevin Bayley, Tania Bering, Evan Copage, John Gerald, Bruce McKinnon, Michael Sabbatino, Edan Epstein and Luke Turalitsch.

I am so blessed for the friendships of Carol Jackson and Justin Christman. Your encouragement keeps me moving in the right direction. I have also been very touched by the gift of art for the book's cover by artist Carrie Gordon. Thank you for capturing the book in art and for turning words into an image I will cherish for a life time.

Dedications

To my four kids, my life would not be complete without the daily gifts of your love. I love you so very much Taylor, Drew, John and Joe.

To my parents, I am so lucky that many moons ago my mom quit her job in Ocean City to run away with my dad. And I am so thankful to be a part of that love story.

PART ZERO

Author's Note: I don't feel the number zero gets the recognition it deserves except on a number line or a thermometer. I believe in stand-up comedy you must start at the absolute beginning that's why this section is Part Zero.

What is Stand-up Comedy?

Hopefully when you purchase a book called The Craft of Stand-up Comedy, you do know something about stand-up comedy. But since this is America, where we put warnings on plastic bags reminding us that it's not a toy, here's a little information on stand-up.

If the good people at Webster's Dictionary were to come up with a definition for stand-up comedy it would probably be;

Stand-up Comedy- the precise use of body language, voice and emotions upon words by a solo performer to invoke laughter within an audience.

Those solo performers they are called comedians of which you are on your way to becoming one .As a teacher of stand-up comedy here is the most important definition I want you to learn. Stand-up comedy is an intimate pre-planned conversation between comedian and audience. The comedian shares opinions, feelings and attitudes based on his/her experiences. During much of the conversation the comedian does the talking and the audience responds by way of laughter.

Is Stand-up Comedy a form of Art?

Most definitely YES.

A great stand-up comedy performance, with the audience whirling in fits of laughter is as worthy as any Picasso, Monet, or Rembrandt hanging in a museum to be called Art.

The definition of Art is a skill acquired by experience, study or observation and the conscious use of that skill along with creative imagination to create. Stand-up comedy lives up to every aspect of that definition George Carlin has my favorite quote on the art of stand-up comedy.

"It seems to me that of all the artist there are- poets, painters, sculptors- the stand-up comedian is the only one who gets to create the work in front of the people it's intended for, allows the people to shape the work through their reaction at the time it's being made."

For some examples of stand-up comedy performances please look-up these great proprietors of the craft of stand-up comedy these artist known to us as comedians;

George Carlin, Richard Pryor, Robin Williams, Eddie Murphy, Billy Crystal, Whoopi Goldberg, Bob Newhart, Louis CK, Bob Hope, George Burns, Lewis Black, Mort Sahl, Sid Caesar, Tom Lehrer, Joan Rivers, Roseann Barr, Woody Allen, Phyllis Diller, Lilly Tomlin, Paula Poundstone, Louie Anderson, Wanda Sykes, Steve Martin, Lenny Bruce, Jerry Seinfeld, David Letterman, Ellen DeGeneres, Don Rickles, Jonathan Winters, Bill Hicks, Johnny Carson, Sam Kinison, Dennis Miller, Steven Wright, Rodney Dangerfield, Jay Leno, Bill Maher, Richard Lewis, Redd Foxx, Milton Berle, Dave Chappelle, Freddie Prinze, Jack Benny, Ray Romano, Robert Klein, Garry Shandling, Denis Leary, Flip Wilson, Andy Kaufman, Tim Allen, Adam Sandler, John Pinette, Margaret Cho, George Lopez, Carrot Top, Daniel Tosh, Buddy Hackett, Jim Carrey, Martin Lawrence, Albert Brooks, Jon Stewart, Henny Youngman, Dave Attell, Damon Wayans, Shelly Berman, Bernie Mac, Drew Carey, Dick Gregory, Norm MacDonald, Dom Irrera, DL Hughley, Bobby Slayton, Jackie Mason ,Richard Belzer, Sinbad, Alan King, David Brenner, Richard Jeni, Cedrick the Entertainer, Red Buttons, Jay Mohr, Bobcat Goldthwait, Kevin Pollak, Billy Connolly ,Robert Schimmel, Pat Cooper, Howie Mandel, Jeff Foxworthy, Eddie Izzard, Kevin James, Brett Butler, Mitch Hedberg, Brian Regan, Kathleen Madigan, Katt Williams, Kevin Hart, Mel Brooks,

Doug Stanhope, Jeff Ross, Paul Mooney, Bobby Lee, Dana Carvey, David Spade, Gabriel Iglesias, Eddie Griffin, Jamie Foxx, Brad Garrett, Natasha Leggero, Chris Hardwick, Kumail Nanjiani, Jonah Ray, Todd Barry, Amy Schumer, Jim Gaffigan, Adam Devine, Jimmy Fallon, Aziz Ansari, Mike Birbiglia, Kyle Kinane, Gabe Liedman, Tracy Morgan, Zach Galifianakis, Rory Scovel, Reggie Watts, Eugene Merman, Keisten Schaal, George Wallace, Sarah Silverman, Ricky Gervais, Joe Mande, Chelsea Peretti, Tig Notaro, Bill Burr, Connan O'Brien, Patton Oswalt, Jeff Dunham, Maria Bamford, Chris D'Elia, Nikki Glaser, Demetri Martin, Hannibal Buress, Marc Maron, Pete Holmes, Joe Rogan, Patrice O'Neal...just to name a few

Stand-up Comedy Needs You

Yes, You.

There are over seven billion people on this planet, and all of them love to laugh. Did you know laughter predates speech by about a million years? And are you aware that as humans laughter is instinctive? A human infant can laugh almost from birth. And people born blind and deaf still laugh. We not only love to laugh, we need to laugh. We've all heard the phrase "Laughter is the best medicine". That phrase is one hundred percent true. Here is a list of what laughter does for us;

Boost Immunity
Lowers Stress Hormones
Decreases Pain
Relaxes Muscle Tension
Prevents Heart Disease
Eases Anxiety
Relieves Stress
Improves Mood
Enhances Resilience

Stand-up comedians are on the front lines of the world's insatiable need to laugh. Stand-up comedians also serve as modern day philosophers easing tension and stress from a world that is confusing and growing more complicated each and every day.

So where do you fit in all this funny business?

Glad you asked.
Every comedian brings to the stage their own individual perspective on life, not a single comedian is going to be able to resonate with all seven billion people. Another way of saying this is not everyone finds the same thing funny. Therefore in order to keep the world's population laughing we need as many different perspectives as possible. We need as many comedians as we can find.

Okay so why you?

Glad you asked that too.
Because you're the only one with your perspective……
Your mind, your opinion, your thoughts, your parents, your cat, your dog, your spouse, your kids,
And so on and so forth.
There is only one person on this Earth just like you. And that is you.
Share with us. And make funny too.

Leave Your Fear Right Here

In the words of FDR" The only thing we have to fear is fear itself". Fear does have another name it's called irrational thoughts. I've performed stand-up comedy for over sixteen years. I still get nervous before every show but I never get scared. The reason I'm not scared is because I know how to suppress irrational thoughts. It's easy and there are only five rules you must remember.

5 Important Tips to Disarm Fear

1 Set Attainable Expectations

Throughout my stand-up comedy career, I have set attainable expectations for myself. I am only expecting ten percent of what I do on stage to be great and I am expecting the other ninety percent to be garbage. I know what you are thinking "wow Julie those are some really low expectations" But here's the deal, setting my expectations so low really sets my creative energy free. And it gives my creative energy the freedom it needs to create. For the most part I always do better than my ten percent expectation. But when I don't do better, I don't spend time feeling bad about it. I don't let irrational thought paralyze me. I "move on" and create more material, practice more and get on with my stand-up comedy.

LOW EXPECTATIONS = CREATIVE FREEDOM

Also a good way to think of this rule is to remember to set your stand-up comedy goals at an attainable rate. Another way of saying this, "Don't plan on having your Comedy Central Spotlight Special next month". Instead a more attainable stand-up comedy goal for you right now would to be ready to perform in your first open mic in six weeks.

Setting realistic goals with your stand-up comedy will also provide more freedom for your creative energy to grow and learn.

2 Set Achievable Dreams

Now I am not saying "Don't dream". Because I believe in dreams. I think if people are willing to work hard they can accomplish anything they have set in their mind. What I am saying is be realistic about what is going to happen when you get on stage. Like I said each and every time I'm about to get on stage, I am nervous. But I have a realistic dream of what is going to happen. And my realistic dream is this:

I know I am going to do my best. I am going to enjoy my moment in the spotlight. I am going to help some of my fellow human beings have a good laugh.

That's it.

I don't allow my mind to have fantasy stand-up comedy sets. I don't imagine a big Hollywood producer coming up to me after my set to offer me a television deal. Instead I imagine audience members coming up to me to thank me and me thanking them.

See that's achievable. If the fantasy happens someday, Great.

Until then, I will enjoy the creative freedom provided to me by having achievable, realistic dreams about being on stage.

3 Celebrate You

Yes, celebrate even the smallest of victories. Okay I agree, it's a sappy rule but a very important one. So hear me out on this.

You are about to embark on the really big task of writing and performing your first stand-up comedy set. Even as you read these words you are on your way to becoming a stand-up comedian. This is a huge task. It even sounds overwhelming. In fact you may even be feeling a little overwhelmed at this point. But here's a little thing I learned from a mentor years ago. Every time I would go to my mentor and explain my overwhelming task. My mentor would just reply "How do you eat an elephant?" I would reply with the answer "one delicious bite at a time" And that's exactly what we are going to do with you. You will become a stand-up comedian one step at a time. And I want you to celebrate each and every step you take towards your stand-up comedy goals.

Celebrate every exercise you accomplish in this book.

Celebrate every set-up.

Celebrate every punch.

Celebrate every joke.

Celebrate every open mic

Celebrate every performance.

Celebrate you, because you are amazing.

4 Never Compare Yourself to Any Other Comedian

Never hold yourself or comedy up to another. You are your own unique person and there is no one quite like you. It would be shame if the world did not get to hear from you because you didn't think you were as good as someone else. Here's a good example. There was a comedian starting out years ago and he admired the work of Lenny Bruce. Now if this comedian would have held his early performances up to the great Lenny Bruce, and decided he wasn't good enough to be a stand-up comedian. Then we would have never heard from George Carlin. Wouldn't that had been a shame? I think so.

And now for the biggest, most important Irrational Thought Suppressor ever......

5 The Audience is on Your Side.

Remember the above sentence as you are waiting to go on stage. It really does help calm that queasy feeling you have right before a performance. And best of all, it's true. Everybody in the audience is rooting for you. They came out to have a good time. And they are looking forward to the laughs you are going to give to them. The audience is on your side. Nobody wants to hurt you. Nobody wants to see you fail. It's a love fest when you're on stage. Enjoy it.

So like this section title, I'm telling you "Leave your fear right here" If you:

Set Attainable Expectations

Set Achievable Dreams

Celebrate Yourself

Never Compare Yourself to Another

Always Remember The Audience is on Your Side

There is nothing to fear. You may get nervous just like me (and every other comedian I know) but that nervous feeling disappears the very moment you get on stage. And the enjoyment you feel from the audience's laughter outweighs the discomfort you felt by about a million tons.

<u>Watch Stand-up Comedy</u>

Roll up your sleeves, let's get ready to work. We are going to do our first assignment. I want you to watch some stand-up comedy. It's very important for this assignment for you to try to pick your favorite comedian. I know that is a daunting task within itself. Because we all like so many different comedians. But I want you to do your best at picking your favorite. Now you need to find about a twenty minute set from your favorite comedian. The internet is an excellent resource for viewing Stand-up comedy performances. You Tube has made stand-up comedy so much more available. Literally any performance from any comedian is right at your fingertips.

Now once you've found that twenty minute set of your favorite comedian. I want you to watch it three times.

On the first time watch and laugh your bottom off.

Before you watch it a second time, read the questions below. Now watch it and notice the information the questions are asking.

Watch it a third time, pen in hand and answer the questions. You might even want to watch the performance more times. The more you watch, the more you notice, the more you notice the more you learn.

Watch Stand-up Comedy Exercise

Name of Comedian_____

What topics did the comedian talk about? List them.

What was the comedian wearing?

Did the comedian do any voices other than their own?

Did you notice the comedian using any facial expressions during their routine?

Did you notice any body language the comedian may have been using during their routine?

Did you notice if the comedian changed the tone of his/her voice during any particular parts of their routine?

Did the comedian use physical action to act out a part of his/her routine?

Did the comedian have any punch lines that totally took you by surprise?

Was there any point in the comedian's set where the facial expression/body language did not match the words being stated?

What subjects did the comedian talk about that you found relatable to your life?

Did the comedian tell any stories during their set? What did they tell stories about?

How did the comedian start their routine?

How did the comedian end their routine?

What is the overall attitude of the comedian during their set?

What impressed you most about this comedian?

Is there anything about this comedian that you did not like?

Write out word for word one joke from this comedian's set. (Please Note: You are never to perform this joke as part of your performance. This is for learning purposes only)

PART ONE

Getting to Knowing Yourself

Okay not that I am saying you don't know you. But What I am saying "Knowing one's self is one of the strongest tool in the stand-up comedian arsenal". And really sometimes we forget about ourselves as we take on roles in life. Example:

When men and women become parents sometimes they forget all about themselves and become wrapped up in their roles as parents. In stand-up comedy you need to cut through all the roles you play and get to the heart of you. Because that heart, that very center of you is going to be doing all the writing, the thinking, and the performing. This next exercise is designed to help clear out the cob webs and help you see the amazing, goofy, wonderful person that is you. This is a long exercise. I recommend you give yourself a few days or even a week to complete. If some of the questions bring a funny story to mind, write it down.

Describe your mother in three words.

Describe your father in three words.

What did your mom do for a living?

What did your dad do for a living?

What is your favorite thing about your mother?

What is your least favorite thing about your mother?

What is your favorite thing about your father?

What is your least favorite thing about your father?

Did your mother ever do anything that embarrassed you in front of your friends?

Did your father ever do anything that embarrassed you in front of your friends?

How did your parents punish you?

How did your parents tuck you in at night?

When you were a kid, were there monsters under your bed?
Did you believe in the Boogie Man?

Does your family have any traditions?

What was your first pet? What was its name?

What is your first memory?

What was your favorite toy as a kid?

What was your favorite piece of playground equipment?

Where did you go to school?

Did you study a lot in school?

What was your favorite subject in school?

Were you popular in school?

Were you ever picked last for a team in Gym class?

Did you ever tattle on anybody?

Did you play an instrument in school? If yes, what did you play?

Do you have any of the same friends you had in grade school?

What is your favorite memory of kindergarten?

What was your favorite grade in school?

Did you ever get suspended from school?

Were you ever a Boy Scout or Girl Scout?

What chores did you have as a kid?

What was your favorite sport as a kid?

How old were you when you learned to tie your shoes?

What was your favorite knock-knock joke as a kid?

What was your favorite cartoon when you were growing up?

What was your least favorite cartoon when you were growing up?

What cartoon character do you think you resemble?

Are you an only child?

Where were you born?

Do you have any birthmarks?

Were you a cry baby?

Did you have any nicknames when you were a kid?

Do you have any brothers and/or sisters? How many of each?

Where are you in the birth order?

Do you remember your first crush?

Do you remember your first kiss? Who was it?

How did your parents tell you about the "Birds and Bees"? How old were you?

Did you ever get caught making out when you were a teenager?

Did your mom ever tell you "You're going to go blind"?

What is on your permanent record? Or what is the worst thing you did as a child?

Are you afraid of the dentist?

Do you prefer the ocean or the mountains?

Have you ever had a reoccurring nightmare?

Do you have a favorite position to sleep?

Are you a night owl or a morning person?

Are you good at returning calls?

What is the dirtiest word in the English language to you?

What is your favorite U.S. city?

What is the meaning of kindness to you?

What does the word "wealth" mean to you?

What is your favorite holiday?

Do you have any bad habits?

Is there anything that you did that makes you feel ashamed?

When you make a mistake, do you admit it?

Would you lie to save someone's feelings?

What do you do to take care of yourself?

Do you keep a diary?

Have you ever lost your composure?

Have you ever been rejected by another person?

What attracts you most to a person of the opposite sex?

What is your favorite comfort food?

What do you like least about yourself?

What do you worry about?

What have you had to "let go of" in your lifetime?

Are you religious?

Is the glass half empty or half full?

Does the thought of getting older scare you?

Do you ever feel overwhelmed? If yes, how do you cope?

Would you say you are a patient person?

How far do you plan ahead?

How did or how would you propose marriage to someone?

Do you ever feel ugly?

Have you ever seen a therapist?

What do you like best about your face?

What do you like least about your face?

Do you like Valentine's Day?

Do you like to give and receive hugs?

Have you ever felt empty?

What is your version of a happy life?

Do you get bummed out at sad movie endings?

Have you ever had a guilty conscious?

Would you consider yourself a liberal or a conservative?

Are you clumsy?

Who is the bravest person you know?

What makes you blush?

Do you have any regrets?

Do you gossip?

Do you like to listen to gossip?

Where do you like to be touched?

Who is the wind beneath your wings?

Are you a litterbug?

Are you a good worker?

How do you amuse yourself when you get stuck in traffic?

Do you make a "to do "list? If yes what was on it today?

Do you sweat a lot?

Do you swear a lot?

What is your favorite toy as an adult?

Can you do math in your head?

Do you smile first?

Do you like to write? If yes what do you write?

What are you going to do when you retire?

Who do you respect the most?

What is a requirement to be your friend?

What is your favorite piece of junk in your house?

What do you hate most about your home?

What is your ethnic background?

Are you happy with your name?

Do you ever lie about your age?

Would you rather be too hot or too cold?

Do you crack your knuckles?

When you stump your toe, do you cry or curse?

Do you like to snuggle?

Are you good with babies?

How many hours of sleep do you need?

Are you friendly with police officers?

What chores around the house do you do now?

Are you a perfectionist?

What is the sexiest music in your opinion?

What is your panic button?

What makes you angry?

What do you do when you are depressed?

What do you do when you are angry?

How do you know when you are nervous?

At the beach, are you in the water or on the shore?

Are you a cat person or a dog person?

Do you have any nutty people in your life?

Has anybody ever described you as a drama queen?

What do you consider your life's work?

Do you swim upstream or downstream?

Do you follow the herd or do you break away from the pack?

In your car, is the radio set to AM or FM?

Do you like sports?

Have you ever been in a fight?

What is the most disgusting thing you ever ate?

What has been your favorite concert?

What was your least favorite employment experience?

What was your most favorite employment experience?

Have you ever been in the hospital?

Have you ever been in a car accident?

Where do you want to go that you haven't been?

What is your favorite news source?

Do you have any trophies?

Have you ever broken any bones?

Do you have a real life ghost story?

What was your worst vacation?

Describe your best friend.

Have you ever gotten even with someone?

Have you ever been boating?

Have you ever went hunting?

Do you ever lie about your weight?

What is the wildest thing you ever done?

Describe the worst place you ever lived.

Have you ever had your fortune read?

Have you ever passed out?

If you were on a deserted island, what is the one thing you would want to have with you?

If you were on a deserted island, who is the one person you would want to have with you?

Would you or do you sky dive?

What is the best party you've ever been?

What is the most stupid thing you have been persuaded to do?

Do you like to travel by airplane?

What is the longest flight you've taken?

Do you vote in election years?

Have you ever ridden a horse?

Would you ever pose nude for a painting?

Have you ever been through an earthquake?

Have you ever had a bad rash?

How many times have you fallen in love?

Have you ever collected unemployment?

Have you ever told a friend's secret?

Have you ever fell asleep at a totally inappropriate time?

Have you ever broke wind at a totally inappropriate time?

Where did you go to college?

What is the bravest thing you have ever done?

What is the most bizarre thing that's happen to you?

Are you a regular anywhere?

Have you ever bought anything from an infomercial?

Have you ever traded something and then wished you could trade it back?

Have you ever traveled by train?

Have you ever went camping?

Have you ever gotten lost?

Have you ever had to serve on a jury?

Have you ever suffered withdraw symptoms?

Do you get car sick?

Have you ever adopted an animal?

Have you ever had to make a speech?

Have you ever screamed really loud?

Have you ever ripped your pants right in the buttocks?

Has someone ever been rude to you?

Have you ever been rude to someone?

Have you or would ever go to a nudist colony?

Do you ever sit outside at night and look at the stars?

Have you ever had a boss that was a tyrant?

When was the last time you were at the doctor's?

Do you know how to roller-skate?

Do you ever go to dive bars?

Have you ever been on a cruise?

Have you ever been to a Drive-in movie?

At amusement parks, what is your favorite ride?

Have you ever stuck your foot in your mouth?

Have you ever stuck you neck out for someone?

Do you go to art galleries?

What is your favorite museum?

Where was the best sunset you have ever seen?

What is the most expensive meal you have eaten?

What is the worst hairstyle on you?

When you go to baseball game, do you stay for the whole game?

Do you still like fireworks?

Have you ever been fishing?

Do you go crazy around the full moon?

Have you ever been on a blind date?

Do you ever break the speed limit?

What is the happiest you've ever been?

Do you like to cook?

What's your favorite meal?

Are you married or have you been or do you plan to be married?

Do you watch TV News reports?

What is your favorite part of a relationship?

What is your least favorite part of a relationship?

What sports do you play?

Do you play any instruments?

What do you do to be kind?

Have you ever won something?

Do you have an entourage?

Do you like to dance?

What is your favorite charity?

What is your favorite drink?

What is your favorite Board game?

What is your favorite cheese?

Do you have any pets? If so what are their names?

Do you floss every day?

What is your favorite kind of shoe?

Do you have any tattoos?

Do you like magic?

What is your favorite marching band instrument?

Do you like roll coasters?

What is your favorite TV Show?

Do you have any kids? How many? What are their ages?

What does your voice mail greeting say?

What is your favorite game to play in Las Vegas?

Do you believe in ghosts?

What is your favorite fruit?

What is your least favorite vegetable?

What is your favorite fairytale?

Zipper or button fly?

Do you like jewelry?

What is your favorite magazine?

Do you have any vision problems?

What is the first thing you do when you wake up in the morning?

Do you collect anything? If so, what do you collect?

Do you take a bath or a shower?

Do you people watch?

How would you end a war?

Do you like guns?

Do you believe marijuana should be legal?

What is your favorite letter of the alphabet?

What do you do to entertain yourself?

Do you have a will?

What is your favorite soft drink?

Would you rather be too hot or too cold?

What do you wear to sleep?

What is your favorite quote?

Who is your favorite writer?

Do you have any phobias?

Do you like to have your picture taken?

Do you have any piercing?

Do you know how to fix anything?

What is your favorite animal at the zoo?

What kind of houses interest you?

Have you ever protested something/

Do you enjoy quiet time?

What type of music do you enjoy?

Who is your favorite rebel?

Have you ever forgotten a loved one's birthday?

Have you ever been caught in a bad storm?

What is your favorite food to eat at a carnival or fair?

Have you ever been overweight?

Do you believe in elves?

Do you think you have the endurance to run a marathon?

What in the world today causes you the most confusion?

Do you have any consultants?

Are you a pack rat?

Are you afraid of clowns?

What is your favorite month?

What is your favorite season?

Do you like bugs?

What is your least favorite bug?

Do you believe in Bigfoot?

Do you know how to swim?

Do you have a green thumb?

Do you know self-defense?

What are you going to do tomorrow?

What are you going to do later tonight?

Do you know any magic tricks?

Do you like to bike ride?

Do you like to go to the dentist?

Do you have a walk in closet?

What is your favorite bird?

Do you like Halloween?

Do you own a Halloween Costume?

What is your favorite beach?

Do you use your cell phone while driving?

Do you like Charmin or Quilted Northern?

Do you exfoliate regularly?

Are you afraid of spiders?

What is your favorite animal at a pet shop?

What is your favorite slang word?

What is your least favorite slang word?

What is your favorite Slurpee flavor?

What is your favorite gum?

Do you know how to blow bubbles with bubble gum?

What is your favorite car?

What kind of car do you drive?

Do you have a scrapbook?

Have you or do you have a mood ring?

Do you like to go bowling?

Are you afraid of snakes?

What is your favorite ice cream flavor?

Do you kill bugs with a bug spray or by stomping them?

Do you have any allergies?

Do you drink bottled water or tap water?

Do you like your beer warm or cold?

What card games do you know how to play?

What is your favorite TV theme song?

What is your favorite part of a news cast?

What is your favorite scary movie?

What is your favorite Chick Flick?

If you could be a guest star on a TV show, which one would it be?

Do you own any flip flops?

If you could be a vegetable, what would you be?

Do you like birds?

Do you recycle?

Do you like your toes?

What is your favorite department store?

What snack do you like to have at the movies?

What is your favorite sandwich?

Do you like to send greeting cards?

What is your favorite football team?

What is your favorite baseball team?

What kind of soap do you use?

What is your favorite kind of pie?

What is your favorite color M&M?

What is your favorite Beatle's song?

Are you a vegetarian?

What is your favorite restaurant?

Whole Life Run Through

Now that the personal interrogation (I mean inventory) is completed, we'll move onward. I hope you had fun and that the questions were able to help you see the marvelous, sensational person inside you. In our next exercise we are going to give ourselves a reminder of what path our lives have taken. Remember in school when the teacher would ask you to write a summary? (Yeah, I totally hated that too,) But don't hate me because this summary is fun and easy. All you have to do is write fifteen sentences that tell others about you. The sentences do not have to follow any type of order. They can be totally random, just as long as they are about you and your life. At the end of this exercise you will have your life summary or your whole life run through.
For example here is mine:

I am a fan of duct tape, the Baltimore Ravens and Coke Cola.

I spent most of my life thinking I was too fat.

I am not a morning person.

I am a nearsighted, left handed, Libra

I lived with someone I hardly knew, for twenty years.

 For ten years, I worked a job that I sometimes liked but most of the time hated.

I fell in love when I was sixteen years old and I never got over it.

My parents were teenagers when they had me, so I got to watch them grow up.

I believe our God is a loving God.

I got to meet and know all four of my grandparents and I miss them every day.

I have been blessed with four children.

I love dogs with pushed in faces.

If I were you, I would not let me drive your car.

I know how to play the violin and I also know how to not play the violin.

Okay now it's your turn

1

2

3

4

5

6

7

8

9

10

11

12

13

14

15

Feelings

Everyone has feelings but comedians know how to turn feelings into laughs. I think it is impossible to go to a stand-up comedy performance and not know how the comedian was feeling about the topics he/she was talking about.

So on to the final frontier of knowing yourself. I hope it doesn't sound too sappy but I want to know how you feel. Or better yet, I want you to have a clearer understanding of your feelings.

Here is a list of words that describe types of feelings.

Happy
Sad
Outraged
Enthusiastic
Disbelieving
Fearful
Hopeful
Disgusted
Confused
Surprised
Depressed
Optimistic
Condescending
Determined

Listed are topics, beside each topic write down words from the feeling word list that best describe your feeling associated with each topic. Then write a brief statement as to why you chose that particular feeling.

Love

Fast Food Restaurants

Global Warming

Teenagers

Beer

Police Officers

Dogs

Shoes

The Bible

Your Mother

Taxes

Automotive Repairs

The Internet

Politics

Your Job

Cell Phones

Football

Your Body

Ping-Pong

Traffic

Facebook

Marijuana

Race

Cyclists

Computers

Your Home

Cigarettes

The Pope

Yard Sales

Doughnuts

Same Sex Marriage

Cats

Education

Tattoos

Crime

What Kind of First Impression do You Make?

Good stand-up comedy involves having a strong sense of self and knowing what's inside your head. But to be a great comedian you need to combine that strong sense of self with an understanding of others. In other words, you need to have an idea of what's going on inside your audience's heads. So far our exercises have been helping us to see what's inside our heads. Now we are going to start looking at what others are thinking. And we are going to start this journey by asking, "What they think of you?" I want you to pick at least three people in your life. Try to pick people that do not live with you. The only exception on that, would be teenage kids. They have no problem with giving you an unfiltered answer. Ask these three people" How would you describe me to someone?" Write down their answers below for safe keeping.

Person number one

Person number two

Person number three

Now that you have an idea what peoples' conceptions or misconceptions, let us take it one step further by answering this question.

<u>What do you try to hide from people when you meet them for the first time? Or phrased this way, what don't you want people to notice about you the first time you meet them?</u> This attribute that you are hiding can be physical or behavioral.

I hope your feelings are not too bruised after doing this exercise. But if they are, we can make that really funny. Also I hope you were able to get some really honest feedback as to how others perceive you. The answers you received here will be great opening topics for your stand-up comedy set.

PART TWO

What Makes Humans Laugh?

In the pursuit of laughter, it is important to know what causes humans to laugh. Chuckles, to belly shaking to on the ground rolling in a fit of laughter has a variety of causes. There are four causes the stand-up comedian needs to know before he/she starts writing jokes.

The number one cause of laughter is surprise and it is present to some degree in all jokes. When the beginning of a joke has the audience's thinking going in one direction, and then the punch line of the joke totally changes that direction. That's a surprise and it leaves the audience in stitches.

Another important laugh generator is Incongruity. When thoughts and actions don't add up, that incongruity creates laughter. Imagine a stand-up comedian talking about how much he loves spending time with his mother in-law with a look of absolute horror across his face. That's incongruent and it's hilarious.

Next on our list of laugh provokers is the old adage "Misery loves company". From the moment the first caveman slipped on the first banana peel gag, pain and an audience's relatable experience to that pain are an unending source of comedy.

Lastly on our list of laugh inducers, we have the Sherlock Holmes effect. That's when an audience is given pieces of a joke throughout a comedian's routine. The audience then puts the pieces together about half a second after the comedian delivers a punch based on those clues. This can also be called a callback if the comedian's punchline is a punchline he/she had used earlier.

There certainly are more causes of why we laugh, but the four listed here seem to be the most prevalent in stand-up comedy. Your stand-up comedy will certainly contain all four of them, overlapping and intersecting at various points throughout your routine.

Stand-up Comedians Must Have Supplies

Believe it or not you have funny thoughts every day. If you are saying to yourself "no I don't have funny thoughts everyday", I can guarantee by the end of Part Two you will have more funny thoughts than you ever thought possible.

First off we need to gather some very important tools of the stand-up comedy craft. They are:

1 Pocket Size Notebooks - You will need several of these notebooks. They fill up fast. Always carry a notebook with you everywhere. Whenever you leave the house be sure to have one with you at all times. I cannot over stress it. You never know when the funny is going to hit the fan. And you want to be sure to capture it, remember it and turn it into a funny bit for your set.

2 Pens - Have pens everywhere. In your car, in your purse, in your bathroom, all over your house pens should be everywhere. You don't want to lose a funny bit because you couldn't find a pen.

3 Voice Recorder(optional) - If you are not a fast writer or you are not a visual person, more of an auditory person, then this item is an absolute must have tool. Luckily most cell phones come with voice recorders as a standard application. This is an excellent tool to capture the funny. And on the plus side of this tool is you are able to capture the tone of the punch as well as the punch itself.

4 Spiral Bound Sketch Pads or any other full size unlined paper pads - These full size pads must be absolutely, positively unlined paper. These full size pads are for taking the funny thoughts you captured in your pocket sized notebook or on your voice recorder and turning them into jokes. The reason they must be unlined paper is because you do not

want anything in the way of your thoughts. You do not want anything that will make your thoughts conform to anything. You want to be able to add in, cross out, write in a bubble, add emotion, write sideways, and whatever and so forth. You need a free range writing space.

Collecting Organic Comedy

There is already a comedian inside you screaming to be heard. Yes, it is true most of your best jokes that you tell on stage are thoughts that came to you naturally as you live your daily life. Your next assignment will be a lifelong assignment. Meaning as long as you plan on being a stand-up comedian, you must always be in the process of this assignment. Your assignment is to carry your pocket size notebook or your voice recorder with you everywhere you go through out your day and to keep it by your bedside at night. And every time you have a funny thought or say something funny (meaning others around you laugh) you need to write it down. Every time something makes you angry or frustrated write it down. Anytime you feel embarrassed, worried or scared write that down too. Every time you feel like punching someone in the face (Don't do that) just write it down. I promise you will get the best of them. It just won't be as messy, but it will be really funny. Before you go any further in this book, I want you to collect at least seven days of funny thoughts, funny things you said, funny incidents, embarrassments, frustrations, and confrontations in your pocket size notebook.

Comedy Writing Suggestions

Writing comedy can be one of the most challenging aspects of stand-up comedy, but it also can be one of the most enjoyable and creative experience of your life. You can take your comedy writing anywhere and everywhere. You can give voices to animals, you can rewrite the Bible or you can even ride a unicorn through downtown Los Angeles. There are no rules when writing comedy, only suggestions.

Suggestion
Be profound in your stand-up comedy and stay away from being labeled as profane.

Now I am not saying don't use profanity ever. What I am suggesting is that you think of profanity as a spice. Add just a little when you need to season the dish. But remember not to use too much because you don't want to overpower the other ingredients in the dish. Keeping profanity to a minimum demonstrates to others you are a creative, innovated, writer/performer and opens up many doors for your stand-up comedy career.

Suggestion
Don't spend all your time in The Cotton Enclosure

Ah, yes sex jokes, these are the easiest of all jokes to write. Because the subject and the uncomfortable feelings associated with the subject are universal. In fact you don't need a comedy class or comedy book to write sex jokes, because these jokes write themselves. Since we are thinking of profanity in terms of spice, let's think of sex jokes in terms of entrée. What if you were to go to an all you can eat buffet and all that was available was chicken. Fried chicken, broiled chicken, roasted chicken, grilled chicken, stir-fry chicken, chicken nuggets, barbeque chicken and so on and so forth. You'd get sick of chicken if you ate that much chicken. That is exactly why you need a variety of subjects in your stand-up comedy. If you tell an audience sex joke, after sex joke, after sex joke, they get tired of sex jokes. Not to mention the comedian that was on stage before you probably had his own brand of sex jokes too. Now I'm not saying take chicken off the buffet altogether. I'm saying be sure you are offering your audience a smorgasbord of items to enjoy when they are being entertained by you.

What is a Joke?

A joke is actually the shortest form of a story. It has a beginning which is called a set-up. It has a middle which is used for building tension. It has an end which is called a punch. Just like a story it starts where it needs to start meaning it only give enough details for the story to be logical. Just like a story a joke has a plot and it ends with a twist of that plot. A joke can be as short as one sentence or it can take as many sentence as needed to get to the punch.

The Set-up and the Middle

The set-up is the beginning of the joke/story and it also contains the middle of the joke/story. It identifies the characters involved in the joke/story. Sometimes the set-up pulls the audience in as part of the joke/story. Have you ever noticed a comedian asking "Have you ever notice?"? Boom, now the audience is a part of the joke/story. Throughout the set-up the comedian builds tension by giving hints to audience about his/her feelings and possible problems involving the subject.

The Punch

The punch happens when the comedy plot twist has been applied to the subject of the story/joke. And if you created a believable authentic set-up and gave just enough details for the punch to work the audience will laugh.

Stand-up Comedy Writing Exercise One

Fill in these set-ups with your punches. You may use more than one word to fill in the blanks.

1 You can lead a horse to water but you can't make him

_____

2 I love writing letters. I even once wrote a letter to

_____

3 Driving in L.A. is like driving

_____

4 Today is a beautiful day. When I see a day like today I think

_____

5 I was talking to my mother the other day. Okay I was talking to
my_____

6 I got my bank statement the other day my balance reminds me of

_____

7 Every time I read the newspaper I think

_____

8 I'm almost scared to take a walk these day. I'm always afraid of

_____

9 It has been said you shouldn't talk about race politics or religion
when you meet someone for the first time. When you meet someone
for the first time I think you should talk about _____ ,
_____ and _____.

10 You know when you get sick and you can't get out of bed. At those
times I'm always thinking

_____

11 My idea of camping is

_____

12 Morning breath is a warning from your mouth. It is trying to tell you_____

Stand-up Comedy Writing Exercise Two

This one is set up to be like a stand-up set. Fill in the set-ups and the punches. You may use as many words as needed to fill in the blanks.

Good Evening, Good Afternoon Whatever........

My name is _____ but you can call me
_____

Usually the first thing people notice about me is
_____. But look closer folks if you really look close you can see I'm
_____.

I really hate my _____ because
_____. Sometimes I wish I could change it to _____ because
_____.

My Mom can be exciting if you like
_____.
Not that I'm saying she is a bad person. But just one look at her and her _____ and you know you're in for it.

My dad on the other hand can be exciting too if you're into

_____

But please don't ask my parents about me because they will just say

_____.

When I was a kid my favorite game was _____. I've always wished I could do that professionally.

When I was growing up I wanted to be a _____ but now I'm a _____. Well at least I still

_____

My co-workers are a nice group of

_____. I love spending 8 hours a day with people who

_____.

I have a pet _____ and I've always wondered "Why people have pets?"
Could it be because we need

_____.

You know what bugs me most about society
is_____. If I was in charge
I'd_____.

Cultivating Your Organic Comedy

So now that you are armed with the knowledge that a joke is actually a small story, it's time to go through the entries you've been collecting in your pocket size notebook. You need to go through your notebook and identify what you have written down.

Do you have the beginning or middle or ending of a joke? Do you have a set-up or do you have a punch? Or do you already have both a set-up and a punch?

Going through Your Pocketsize Notebook

Take a moment and go through the entries in your pocket size notebook one entry at a time.

If an entry has both a set-up and a punch put the letter J beside that entry. It's already a joke and needs no cultivation.
If the entry is just a set-up and has no punch, put the letter S beside it.
If the entry is a punch and you need to develop a set-up for it, put the letter P beside it.

Turning Punches into Jokes

Let us start with the entries that have the letter P beside them. These are actually very easy to turn into jokes. They are punches. They are the endings of the jokes/stories. Most stories are written backwards meaning the writer knows the ending before he begins to write. Remember that sketch notebook with unlined paper, write down one of your entries with the letter P on a blank page in that notebook. As the writer of this joke you have to ask yourself "What details to I need to reveal in order for this ending/punch to be logical? The answer to that question is the set-up for this joke. When asking yourself this question I suggest you might want to use a bubble map. That means jotting down key words as they pop in to your head put a circle around each word to create a bubble. That takes the initial pressure of forming sentences off your shoulders and opens up your creativity. Once you have key words then you can place them in logical order to form your set-up.

Turning Set-ups into Jokes

Now that you know how to write a joke backwards. It's time to progress to writing a joke forwards. Chance are the entries with the letter S beside them are funny thoughts, ideas, funny topics, but they are going to need work to transform them into jokes. Transfer an entry with the letter S onto a blank page in your sketch book. You start processing this entry by asking yourself "What is the subject/topic of this entry?" Write that subject/topic in a bubble. Then proceed by asking yourself "What feelings do I have about this subject/topic?" Again use a bubble technique, do not force yourself to write complete sentences. Establishing your feelings about the subject/topic does not necessarily mean you have to say your feeling word in your set-up. It is more possible you will be showing your feelings through the tone of your voice, facial expressions and movements during the delivery of your joke.

Introduction to the 8 Questions of Comedy Writing

The next part of the comedy cultivation process is the applying of comedy plot twist onto your subject by asking yourself a series of eight questions. These eight question are designed to help you look at the topic from all different angles and create multiple joke possibilities. Now granted some of the eight questions may produce answers that overlap or intersect that is a natural part of comedy writing. Try to stay with the process and ask all eight questions before settling on one joke because you may get many jokes that you can use in your set. I have presented each question one at a time and also provided an example In the following section there are detailed exercises for each of the comedy questions to help you explore this mode of comedy writing. . The subject/topic I picked for the example was being a PTA President, it was a part of my life I've never explored the comedy involved in it .My feeling that I attached to it was bittersweet.

1 Can I tell my truth about this subject?

My Example:

I was a PTA President for three years. It was some of the most boring, unfulfilling, dissatisfying years of my life. I miss it so……

2 Can I use sarcasm and tell a lie about this subject?

My Example:

I actually like all the pomp and circumstance and power connected with the position. Plus music would play every time I walk into room. (Sing) If you're happy and you know it (angry voice) go away

3 Can I compare this subject to something relatable or totally un- relatable?

My Example:

Running the PTA was a lot like running my house. No matter what I did there was always at least one unhappy camper.

Running the PTA was a lot like trying to give the cat a bath, no matter how good your intentions are....you're still going to get hurt.

4 Can I put this subject somewhere where it doesn't belong or can I put something with this subject that wouldn't naturally be there?

My Example:

It was always hard getting the other parents to volunteer to help .I think it's because I was too nice The principal always blamed it on the language barriers. That's why I think all PTA presidents should get their training from the Mafia. Because brass knuckles and busted knee caps is a language we can all understand.

5 Can I be totally inappropriate in my thoughts/opinions about this subject?

My Example:

The hardest thing for me to deal with was the other PTA Presidents. What an uptight group of overbearing coupon clipping whack jobs.

6 Can I use a "play on words" with this subject?

My Example

I think PTA actually stands for Parental Tension Association.

I had never seen so many uptight people in one place at the same time.

7 Can I use my imagination and apply a "What if?" scenario to this subject?

My Example:

Our PTA raised all the money to pay for P.E. and art classes. As much as the PTA got on my nerves, I'd hate to see our kids without them. Because if we think they are fat and ignorant now……..you might as well just have a class called "Would you like fries with that?

8 Can I tell a story about this subject?

My Example:

Being a PTA President I always got calls from the school about my children, status updates if you will….Anyhow so I answer the phone and all I can hear in the background is my youngest son saying "It's broken, I keep telling you it's broken. It's broken". The principal proceeds to tell me that young Joseph has gotten into a fight on the playground with another boy. Joseph interrupts from the background with another "It's broken" and then starts to cry. The principal continues to tell me she had to call the other boy's mother and that the other boy has went home early because he is afraid of your magic wand. Again Joseph is sobbing" It's broken why doesn't anyone believe me?" The principal goes on "Apparently you have a magic wand at your house and Joseph told the other boy he was going to use it to turn him into an amphibian. But I understand it's broken so I guess we don't have to worry about that" I thanked her for the call but I got off the phone thinking that wand is not broken.

The 8 Questions of Comedy Writing Exercises

1 Can I tell my truth about this subject?

Is my truthful experience or my truthful opinion associated with subject funny?

There is a formula in comedy that goes like this Truth + Pain = Laughs. This formula works because you are showing to the audience you are in fact very human. The second reason it works goes back to the old saying "Misery loves company", an audience is always happy to know that your life is just as imperfect as theirs.

Truthful Comedy Writing Exercise

In the chart below next to the subject write one of the feeling words that best describe your feelings about the subject. In the next column write a truthful statement based on your feeling and experience with the subject

Feeling words: Happy, Sad, Outraged, Enthusiastic, Disbelieving, Fearful, Hopeful, Disgusted, Confused, Surprised, Depressed, Optimistic, Condescending,. And Determined

SUBJECT	FEELING ATTACHED	STATEMENT ABOUT SUBJECT USING FEELING
Kids	Confused	It's easier to send a man to the moon than to raise a well-balanced child.

Family		
Food		
Pets		

2 Can I use sarcasm and tell a lie about this subject?

When you tell a lie in comedy, you are basically telling the truth. Although the words that come out of your mouth will be a lie, it is the sarcastic tone with which it is delivered that lets the audience know what is in fact authentic.

Using Sarcasm to Tell a Lie Writing Exercise

In the chart below next to the subject write one of the feeling words that best describe your feelings about the subject. In the next column write the opposite of the feeling you have attached to the subject. In the next column write a truthful statement based on your opposite feeling and experience with the subject

Feeling words: Happy, Sad, Outraged, Enthusiastic, Disbelieving, Fearful, Hopeful, Disgusted, Confused, Surprised, Depressed, Optimistic, Condescending, And Determined

Subject	Feeling Attached	Opposite Feeling	Statement based on the Opposite feeling
Kids	Confused	Understanding	Kids are easy, once you figure out it is the yellow M&Ms that make them misbehave.
Family			
Food			
Pets			

3 Can I compare this subject to something relatable or totally un- relatable?

Comparing your subject to another like subject or unlike subject is a great way to share with an audience how you feel about the subject, without even telling them the feeling word attached to it. The audience will begin to connect the dots as your comparison unfolds.

Comedy Comparison Writing Exercise

In the chart below next to the subject write what would make a good comparison for this subject. The item you pick for the comparison can be a person, place, thing, or a situation. In the next column connect the dots between the subject and your comparison by answering the question "Why are they similar?"

Subject	Comparison	Why?
Kids	A Detour	Kids are like a detour because nothing goes as planned.
Family		
Food		
Pets		

4 Can I put this subject somewhere where it doesn't belong or can I put something with this subject that wouldn't naturally be there?

Putting things where they don't belong is called contrasting. (And you thought it was lazy and irresponsible) Contrasting is basically an ambush on the audience. You want them to be surprised by what elements you have put with your subject.

Comedy Contrast Writing Exercise

In the chart below next to the subject write a place where you wouldn't normally find the subject or write an item you would not normally associate with the subject. In the next column write the hilarious result of the subject and its contrast.

Subject	Someplace or something that does not belong with the subject	What would happen?
Kids	Working as a Bartender	Kids would make great bartenders because no matter how crappy you told them your day had been, they would still reply with a "Wow I can't wait till I grow up
Family		
Food		
Pets		

5 Can I be totally inappropriate in my thoughts/opinions about this subject?

Do you have thoughts or opinions that others might frown upon involving this subject? Another way to look at this is to think about your audience's frame of reference to this subject and write down things that they may be thinking but would never say out loud.
Inappropriate Thoughts/Opinions Writing Exercise
Next to each subject write down those improper, unseemly and maybe even unbecoming thoughts or opinions you have about the subject. It

might help for you to remember the feeling you have associated with the subject. Ready, set, be inappropriate!

Subject	What should you not say at a job interview about this subject?
Kids	It's easy to keep kids quiet. All it takes is a couple of well-placed pieces of duct tape and they are as quiet as can be.
Family	
Food	
Pets	

6 Can I use a "play on words" with this subject?

A play on words is when you apply a comedic quirk on a familiar saying, metaphor, famous quote, antonyms, synonyms, homonyms and hyperboles.

Grammar School Review

Antonyms- a word with a meaning that is the opposite of another word

Example: Hot – Cold

Old – Young

Balance – Imbalance

Synonyms- a word that has the same meaning as another word in the same language

Example: polite, courteous, cordial

Funny, amusing, comical, laughable

Comedian, humorist, jokester, quipster

Homonyms- a word pronounced the same as another but different in meaning whether spelled the same way or not.

Example: Blue-blew

Flea-flee

Tow-toe

Hyperbole- language that describes something as better as or worse than it really is

Example: It's raining cats and dogs.

I am so hungry, I could eat a horse.

She never stops talking.

Also keep in mind popular social media phrases, song, book, and movie titles are excellent candidates for a play on words. In order to find a play on words you need to ask yourself a series of questions.

Questions	Example Topic Kids	Pick one Topic Family Food Pets
Are there any other words that have the same meaning as your topic word? Think Synonyms	Children Youngsters Brats	
Does your topic word have any other meaning? Think Homonyms	Baby goats	
What is the opposite of your topic word? Think Antonyms	Senior Citizens Geezers Parents	
Is there a hyperbole that describes your feelings about your topic words? Think Exaggerated	My kids are eating me out of house and home.	
What words rhyme with your topic word?	Bid, fib, lid, Squid, rid	
Is there a popular Ad slogan that describes your feelings about this topic?	Sometimes you feel like a nut, sometimes you don't	
Is there a popular saying or quote that describes your feelings about this topic?	Dammed if you do, dammed if you don't	
Is there a song, book or movie title that describe your feelings about this topic?	AC/DC's Highway to Hell Little Miss Sunshine	
Is there a metaphor that describes your feelings about this topic?	Love conquers all.	

Looking at the suggestions contained in the chart, see how many you are able to turn into jokes.

Example Play on Word Jokes

Kids are great. I know some people call them brats...at least I do. But I have to wonder, when did we start naming them after a Subaru?

I would go as far to say I have a herd of kids. Except we can't milk any of them.

Having children, I have to tell you, sometimes you feel like a nut and sometimes you don't have the parenting skills of a tuna fish.

Parenting for me, is like being on the Highway to Hell with Little Miss Sunshine, you're dammed if you and doomed if you don't.

But one thing my kids have taught me is that most of the time I am right even when I am wrong and that love really does conquer all, even giant squid.

Now it is your turn to play with your words.

7 Can I use my imagination and apply a "What if?" scenario to this subject?

"What if?" is one of the most enjoyable writing techniques. Be prepared to explore a vast territory of the creative license. Using the "What if?" technique allows you to apply an infinite number of comedic quirks to your subject. Such as:

What if the dog could talk? What would he say?

 What if you could exchange roles with the dog? What would that be like?

 What if dogs did not exist? What would the world be like without them?

The only limitation in the "What if" writing technique is your imagination.

"What if?" Writing Exercise

In the second column, in the chart below write the "What if?" scenario you would like to apply to the subject. In the next column write what you imagine the ending result would be for such a scenario.

Subject	Comedic "What if?" Scenario	Ending "What if?" Result
Kids	What if kids could tell you exactly how to raise them?	They would be telling us, "No, No, No don't spank me now. Let me wait a few hours it will be more effective."
Family		

Food		
Pets		

8 Can I tell a story about this subject?

Do you have a funny story or a story that could be made funny about **Family, Food or Pets?** Use the chart below to help craft your comedy story

Beginning of Story	What details are needed in this story?	What is the "Beginning" of your story?
Being a PTA President I always got calls from the school about my children, status updates if you will….Anyhow so I answer the phone and all I can hear in the background is my youngest son saying "It's broken, I keep telling you it's broken. It's broken". The principal proceeds to tell me that young Joseph has gotten into a fight on the playground with another boy. Joseph	Principal calling me Joseph sobbing **What details are not needed for this story?** Number of years I was PTA President. Joseph age The name of the school The name of the other	

interrupts from the background with another "It's broken" and then starts to cry. The principal continues to tell me she had to call the other boy's mother and that the other boy has went home early because he is afraid of your magic wand. Again Joseph is sobbing" It's broken why doesn't anyone believe me?"	boy	
Middle of Story The principal goes on "Apparently you have a magic wand at your house and Joseph told the other boy, he was going to use it to turn him into an amphibian. But I understand it's broken so I guess we don't have to worry about that".	**Which sentence contains the set-up or comedy twist that will provide the punch line?** But I understand it's broken so I guess we don't have to worry about that.	**What is the "Middle" of your story?**
End of Story I thanked her for the call but I got off the phone thinking that wand is not broken.	Congratulations on writing a funny stand-up comedy story	**What is the "Ending" (punch line) of your story?**

Comedy Shorthand

Organizing your material to create your comedy set can be a daunting task. And it is important to remember your stand-up routine is not meant to be read by anybody except you. Chance are as you develop your joke writing techniques, you will also develop your own stand-up shorthand. All of my jokes can be brought to my mind by a one or two word prompt. As you are writing your jokes think of one word or a simple phase that will help you recall that joke when you are on stage performing. Here are examples of my comedy shorthand with jokes I wrote on Kids and Being PTA President. See if you can tell which shorthand goes with which joke.

Unhappy Camper

Boring, unfulfilling, dissatisfying

Kiddie Bartender

Giant Squid

Would you like Fries with that?

Parental Tension

Yellow M&M

Detour

Kiddie Duct Tape

Happy and You know it

Mafia PTA

My Broken Wand

No No Spank me Later

Comedy Writing Suggestion

<u>The Rule of Three</u>

I know. I know. I said that I would only give you suggestions when teaching you comedy writing. So with that being said, I suggest you check out the rule of three. Chances are if you ask a stand-up comedian for their favorite number. Their reply would be three. Why? Because the comedian knows that is the magic number. That is the number that creates tension and that is the number that releases laughter.

So what exactly is
The Rule of Three?

1 When you are giving more than one verb or descriptive adjective, always give three.
2 When you are going to give more than one comparison or contrast, always give three.
3 When you are giving more than one punch on the same set-up, always give three.

So that's the Rule of Three, now here are some suggestions involving the number three

1 Never tell more than three jokes on the one subject in a given performance.
2 Never spend more than three minutes on a given theme.
3 The only time to really break Rule of Three is when you really break it and go to the extreme exaggeration

Rule of Three Exercises

List one Thing I might find in your refrigerator (Example- Old pizza with the olives picked off)

1 _____

List three imaginary items hiding in your refrigerator(Example- 1976 Ford Pinto driver)

1 _____

2_____

3 _____

Put your imaginary items in order below.

Funny_____

More Funny_____

Most Funny_____

Now use them in the order you have them listed above to add the Punch to this Set-up.

One thing I have noticed about people or maybe I should say myself, is that we spend way too much time staring into our refrigerators, I don't know what we are hoping to find maybe

_____Funny

_____More Funny

_____Most Funny

But instead there is only

_____Real Refrigerator Item

It's all Descriptive

Comedians are master at description. It is very important for the audience to know what the comedian is taking about and how the comedian feels about that subject. Our audiences like to piece things together, it adds to the tension. One way to express how you feel about a certain subject without actually stating how you feel is to pick adjectives to describe that subject.
In an earlier exercise you were given a list of works and you were asked to put a feeling word beside it. In this exercise I want you to try to think of three adjectives to describe the word.

Love

Fast Food Restaurants

Global Warming

Teenagers

Beer

Police Officers

Dogs

Shoes

The Bible

Your Mother

Taxes

Automotive Repairs

The Internet

Politics

Your Job

Cell Phones

Football

Your Body

Ping-Pong

Traffic

Facebook

Marijuana

Race

Cyclists

The Pope

Yard Computers

Your Home

Cigarettes

Sales

Doughnuts

Same Sex Marriage

Cats

Education

Tattoos

Crime

Creating Bits

You've got jokes and hopefully you are writing new jokes down every day. Now we need to organize those jokes into a set. Organizing your material to create a set list can be a daunting task. But we are going to break it down into a very do-able process. First if you haven't been using your comedy shorthand to title your jokes take a moment to do that now.

Let us start by grouping like or similar subject jokes together to create a bit. For example in my stand-up set I want to have a bit about dogs. I would look at all my jokes about dogs and pick out my best 3 jokes involving dogs. I would take those 3 jokes about dogs and arrange them in order of funny, more funny and most funny dog joke to create me bit on dogs. Suppose you don't have multiple jokes on a subject such as dogs, but you do have one joke on dogs that you would like to use in your set. Is there another group you could assign that joke such as your home life? Or your friends?

<u>Creating Bits Exercise</u>

Write down your bit title/grouping subject in the space provided. Using your comedy shorthand list the three jokes for this bit in this order #1 Funny, #2 More Funny and #3 Most Funny

Here are my examples using the jokes I wrote on kids and being PTA president.

Bit Title	Kids
#1 Kiddie Duct Tape	
#2 No No Spank Me Later	
#3 Kiddie Bartender	

Bit Title	PTA President
#1	Parental Tension
#2	Would you like fries with that?
#3	My Broken Wand

Bit Title	
#1	
#2	
#3	

Bit Title	
#1	
#2	
#3	

Bit Title	
#1	
#2	
#3	

Bit Title
#1
#2
#3

Bit Title
#1
#2
#3

Bit Title
#1
#2
#3

Bit Title
#1
#2
#3

Organizing Your Set

Once you have your jokes organized into bits, you can arrange those bits together to form your set. When you arrange your bits, it is important to remember that stand-up comedy is a conversation with the audience. So think of a conversation with a complete stranger, after an introduction that conversation typically starts something you are both noticing. That something you are both noticing could be a current event, or the comedian that was on stage before you or maybe something you didn't want them to notice about yourself. In a great conversation as well as a great stand-up comedy set you give people an opportunity to get to know you. And as your stand-up comedy set progresses you can get more personal in your material.

Here is a chart that will help you structure your set. Using the cue questions arrange your bits to form your set. In the first section of your set you want to have your second strongest bit. Hopefully this will be something about you that the audience is noticing or something you don't want them to notice. You don't want it to be your funniest, you want to save your funniest bit for last so you can leave the audience in stiches. In your second part of your set would be a good time to put in bits that talk about what you do for a living or activities that interest you. The next section of your set would be a good time to talk about the people you have relationships, such as spouse, kids, pets, or bosses. In this section it's nice to give to the audience an idea how well or not well you play in the sandbox that is called life. The final section of your set needs to end with your funniest bit. This is your no fail bit, the bit that gets laughs every time you perform it.

Who Are You? 2nd Most Funniest Bit

What Do You Do?

With Whom Do You Have Relationships?

What Are Your Funniest Bits?

Making Transitions

Sometimes it can be overwhelming for a beginning comedian to think of how they are going to make the transition from one subject to another. When you ask a professional comedian how to make transitions in subjects they will reply "you just do". And it's true. You make transitions/ or topic changes every day in the conversations you have with the people in your life. You just don't notice them because it's something so natural you do it without thinking about it.

So let us take a moment to notice some of the phrases we use to make a transition from one subject to another. Here are some examples of transitional phrases

Today I noticed...

Yesterday I noticed...

Have you ever wondered...

Last night I dreamed...

Do you ever have the same recurring nightmare???

I shouldn't be telling you this...

Don't you hate it when...

You'll never guess what happen to me...

Take a moment to write down some transitional phrases you use every day.

Transitional Phrases

Another great transition technique is to let the laughter die completely down, let the room go silent for a beat, then begin your next joke topic. Also feel free to just start your next joke topic and after a few words in, acknowledge to the audience that you have changed the subject. Remember when you are thinking transitions, don't get overwhelmed. We are all adults here, and we are expecting you to change topics.

PART THREE

How to Test Material

So by this point you should have jokes written, and like most stand-up comedians, you're wondering if they are funny. You are ready to test them out. I personally use three different techniques to put jokes to the test.

The first technique is I have several people in my life who I value their opinion when it comes to comedy. They are family and friends in my life who make me laugh. I can test out jokes on them. If they laugh I keep the joke. If they say something that makes the joke funnier, I keep that too.

The second way I test out jokes is a little on the sneaky side. I have been known to slip my jokes into conversations with unsuspecting people. Yes, of course, I have to manipulate conversation topics to get to the subject I need to tell my bit. But such is the life of a comedian. The third method for testing out your jokes is to perform them for an audience. The audience will let you know if your comedic instinct was correct.

Practicing Your Set

Being a new comedian you are probably going to want to try to remember your stand-up set word for word. My advice to you is to squash that desire. Instead when you are practicing focus more on remembering the order of your bits and the basic concepts contained in your jokes. Remembering your jokes this way gives your performance a natural flow compared to the mechanical flow that goes along with memorizing your set word for word.

My favorite practice scenario is having the house to myself, so I can verbally go over my set till I am satisfied. Also a long car ride alone is another great practice space. You will need to make time to verbally go over your routine, but you can also go over your routine in your mind anytime or anyplace.

If you have a show coming up, plan on doing your largest amount of practicing the day before the show .Practicing too much the day of a performance only overwhelms your nerves. Plus doing the bulk of your practicing the day before the show allows for a good night sleep and all your jokes can make their way into your subconscious and become a part of you.

Open Mics

One way to get your jokes in front of an audience, would be to participate in an open mic at a local coffeehouse or comedy club. But please do not use an open mic audience reaction as an indicator as to whether a joke is funny or not funny. And let's take that one step further, do not ever use the audience's reaction at an open mic to decide if you are funny or not funny. If there was ever a moment to believe the line 'It's not you it's them", this is that moment. Most audience members of any given open mic are performers themselves. So chances are while you are on stage pouring your heart and soul into your jokes, audience members will be too lost in their own thoughts to give you attention or laughs. But open mics are a part of the stand-up comedy process and fosters two important stand-up comedy cornerstones: Confidence and Articulation

Open mics provide you with an opportunity to get on stage with an audience. And the more you get on stage, the easier it gets to get on stage. The easier that becomes the more confidence you gain. The more confidence you have in your stage presence, your ability to relax the audience increases. The more relaxed an audiences feels translates into bigger laughs for the comedian at a real comedy show situation. Also open mics provide great opportunities for you to practice articulation. The art of speaking clearly takes practice. Being articulate is important to stand-up comedy. If an audience misunderstands or worst yet can't hear one word, you could lose a whole joke. And if that happens more than once during your routine you will be losing audience members. They will do something else better (check their phone or go to the restroom) to fill up the time, than try to strain to understand what is being said.

Sometimes when I do an open mic I get laughs, but most of the time I get silence mixed with polite smiles. I never judge myself based on an open mic performance. And I cannot stress enough you shouldn't either. Instead let's be grateful for the practice and the opportunity to enhance our delivery.

The Three Secret Ingredients of Stand-up Comedy Performance

So by now you are on your way, you have made tremendous progress .You've taken your unique view of world, written jokes based on that view and have started to practice and perform your own brand of Stand-up Comedy. As you are assembling your comedy arsenal it's time to start thinking about the details that will take your comedy performance to the next level. There are three secret ingredients that you can add to the performance of your well written, funny joke and make it absolutely hilarious.

Voices

The first very powerful addition you can add to your performance is to incorporate voices into your routine. Incorporating voices into your routine means to give the people or things that you are talking about, a voice. Let's say you're telling a joke about your mother, it adds laughs to the joke when you try to impersonate her. Of course your voice will be nothing like hers or maybe it will be dead on. Both ways you shared with the audience what your mom sounds like to you and that's what makes it funny. This ingredient is so powerful because with the use of your imagination you can add a voice to anything. You can give your dog a voice, your car can talk to you or other cars or maybe you can share that conversation you had with that meatball sandwich over lunch. Using a voice that isn't your own takes practice, not so much for the perfection of the voice (remember we are doing comedy) but more for the transition from your regular voice to the subject's voice.

Practice Voices Exercise

It is okay to do this exercise by yourself but it is also great fun to do this exercise with friends and family. Go through this list and try to come up with a voice for each of these characters

YOUR MOTHER

YOUR FATHER

MAFIA GUY

TV ANNOUNCER

SOUTHERN BELLE

 A BRIT

A CAT

A DOG

THE OPPOSITE SEX

AN AIRHEAD

A SNOB

A POTHEAD
A DRUNK
A NICE CHILD
A SPOILED BRAT
A NERD
A VERY OLD WOMAN
A VERY OLD MAN

Incorporating Voices Exercise

Go through your jokes and identify opportunities to add voices. Write down the voices and what the voices will be saying. You can get started by putting three of them here.

1 What is the voice?
What will the voice be saying?

2 What is the voice?
What will the voice be saying?

3 What is the voice?
What will the voice be saying?

Action

Now that you are well on your way to incorporating voices into your routine, you are ready to start investigating the next secret ingredient. That ingredient is action. Some comedians call this secret "Acting Out" because you acting out your joke for the audience. Other comedians call this secret "Taking Them There" which is using your action so that the audience can experience the event /subject as you experienced it. Either way you slice it, it is action.

Example: Let's say you are trying to relate to an audience how your dog drags you down the street every evening like he's on his way to Hometown Buffet. Showing an audience how you look being dragged down the street by a Chihuahua will make a funny image into a hilarious one. Adding action takes practice and a willingness to experiment and exaggerate.

Practice Action Exercise

Try your best to act out the scenarios below. Keep in mind if you were on stage performing you would not necessarily want to be all over the stage. Try to keep all action center stage. Just like the voices exercise, this is a fun group activity. But if you don't have a group, that's okay too. You can do these exercises in front of a mirror. I want you to go through the list twice the first time you act out the scenario do it without sound. On the second run thru add sound.

You driving

Your mother driving

Your father driving

You in a crowd trying to fit in.

You getting pulled over by a police officer

A dogs reaction when it's owner comes home.

You speed walking your way to Olympic Gold

You eating something that taste horrible

You being eaten by a shark

You stepping on something pointy

You knocking on a door

You opening the door

You going thru the door

Your mother knocking on a door

Your mother opening the door

Your mother going thru the door

Your father knocking on a door

Your father opening the door

Your father going thru the door

Incorporating Action Exercise

Go through your jokes and identify the opportunities to add action. Write down the action, what you will be saying and what voice you will be using while doing this action. You can start by writing three of them here.

1 What is the action?

What will you be saying while doing this action?

Will you be using a voice other than your own?

2 What is the action?

What will you be saying while doing this action?

Will you be using a voice other than your own?

3 What is the action?

What will you be saying while doing this action?

Will you be using a voice other than your own?

Feelings

So far you've experienced how the addition of voices and action will improve your performance. Our next secret ingredient is the glue that will hold the whole performance together. Feelings is that glue. In fact that is really the jest of Stand-up Comedy, comedians sharing feelings. It's the audience relating to comedians feelings that creates laughter. We express our feelings several different ways. Of course the most obvious way is just simply use your words to state your feelings. The other ways we express our feelings during our performance are through facial expressions, body language and vocal tone. I am sure you have heard the phrase "A picture is worth a thousand words". When you add the proper or improper facial expressions, body language and tone to your performance. You've done just that, you have added a thousand words to your performance making your joke go even further.

Practice Feelings Exercise

Do the following exercises in front of a mirror. Using only your facial expression express the following feelings. Write down beside each feeling what facial quirks you notice about your face when you are displaying that feeling.

Happy

Sad

Outraged

Enthusiastic

Disbelieving

Fearful

Hopeful

Disgusted

Confused

Surprised

Depressed

Optimistic

Condescending

Determined

Now that we have the facial expression for each feeling, it is time to add the body language. In front of a mirror while doing the facial expression for each feeling add the body language for each one too. Write a brief description of your body language for each feeling.

Happy

Sad

Outraged

Enthusiastic

Disbelieving

Fearful

Hopeful

Disgusted

Confused

Surprised

Depressed

Optimistic

Condescending
Determined

We have the facial expressions and the body language for each feeling, now it's time to add the vocal tone. Again it is helpful to do this exercise in front of a mirror. This time as you go through the list of feeling words doing both the facial expression and the body language for each one.
 I want you to say this line
"I can't believe this is happening to me"
with the proper tone of voice for each feeling. Write down what you notice about your voice while doing each feeling.
Happy
Sad
Outraged
Enthusiastic
Disbelieving
Fearful
Hopeful
Disgusted
Confused
Surprised
Depressed
Optimistic
Condescending
Determined

Another successful way to incorporate feelings into your performance is to show the opposite feeling you are stating. This incongruence creates big laughs. And by adding this component to your stand-up comedy you will soon learn that sometimes it is what is not stated that becomes funny.

Incorporating Feelings Exercise

Go through your jokes and write down the feelings you talk about during your routine. Write down ways you could add facial expression, or body language or vocal tone to enhance this feeling or should you use the opposite facial expression, body language or vocal tone to create an incongruence. You can start by putting three of them here.

1 What is the feeling?
How are you going to express this feeling?
Would it be funnier to express the opposite of this feeling?

2 What is the feeling?
How are you going to express this feeling?
Would it be funnier to express the opposite of this feeling?

3 What is the feeling?
How are you going to express this feeling?
Would it be funnier to express the opposite of this feeling?

Now these secret ingredients are not something you have to keep all to yourself. Feel free to share them with all your comedy friends. And remember anytime you have a joke that you felt didn't work quite the way you had intended, you can always check:

Can I add a voice?

Is there an opportunity to add action?

Are my feelings and emotions clear and well defined?

If you incorporate these three ingredients to your comedy set, I can guarantee you will set yourself apart and be ahead of the comedy herd.

Timing

I am sure you have heard people say the quote Comedy is all about the timing or in comedy timing is everything. But what does that all mean? What is timing?

Timing is the pace at which you deliver your comedy act. Finding your comedic pace is easy. Let's go back to the fact that stand-up comedy is a conversation between the comedian and the audience. With this fact in mind, I want you to start noticing your normal pace of conversation with your friends. This relaxed, friendly, and confident pace should be the same pace you deliver your stand-up comedy set. Once you know your comedic pace you can adjust it to create tension. You are able to enhance the tension within a joke by slowing down just a tad as you are building the set-up. Another big tension booster is stopping and taking a moment (known as a "beat") before delivering the punchline.

Stage Persona

As your comedic timing develops so will your stage persona. Hopefully your stage persona will be reflective of your authentic personality. You will know the moment that happens because you well finally be in the moment. The voice you hear inside your head will be the same voice the audience hears through the microphone. You will no longer be worrying if you are standing in the right place, holding the microphone correctly or remembering your next line. With time and practice you gain the experience to boost your confidence so you can truly be in the moment. Be good to yourself and give yourself the time you need to develop.

Sharing the Stage with YOU

Stand-up comedy is a life long journey and I hope you continue to make your way down this path. There will be ups, downs, hills, valleys, plateaus, and peaks. Oh and did I mention the weather sometimes you are hot other times cold. The important thing to remember is to keep moving forward. Go to open mics, organize comedy shows, keep writing new material, and never stop learning. And please keep in touch, you can reach me at juliehahaheehee@gmail.com

Love, Hugs and Punches

Julie Sandoval

www.ingramcontent.com/pod-product-compliance
Lightning Source LLC
Chambersburg PA
CBHW081234090426
42738CB00016B/3297